Give It a Try!

Kelly Doudna

Consulting Editor Monica Marx, M.A./Reading Specialist

Published by SandCastle™, an imprint of ABDO Publishing Company, 4940 Viking Drive, Edina, Minnesota 55435.

Printed in the United States.

Credits
Edited by: Pam Price
Curriculum Coordinator: Nancy Tuminelly
Cover and Interior Design and Production: Mighty Media
Photo Credits: Brand X Pictures, Comstock, Corbis Images, ImageState, PhotoDisc

Library of Congress Cataloging-in-Publication Data

Doudna, Kelly, 1963-
    Give it a try! / Kelly Doudna.
      p. cm. -- (Sight words)
    Includes index.
    Summary: Uses simple sentences, photographs, and a brief story to introduce six different words: before, boy, give, is, many, the.
    ISBN 1-59197-469-0
    1. Readers (Primary) 2. Vocabulary--Juvenile literature. [1. Reading.] I. Title. II. Series.

PE1119.D67574 2003
428.1--dc21

2003050315

SandCastle™ books are created by a professional team of educators, reading specialists, and content developers around five essential components that include phonemic awareness, phonics, vocabulary, text comprehension, and fluency. All books are written, reviewed, and leveled for guided reading, early intervention reading, and Accelerated Reader® programs and designed for use in shared, guided, and independent reading and writing activities to support a balanced approach to literacy instruction.

Let Us Know

After reading the book, SandCastle would like you to tell us your stories about reading. What is your favorite page? Was there something hard that you needed help with? Share the ups and downs of learning to read. We want to hear from you! To get posted on the ABDO Publishing Company Web site, send us e-mail at:

sandcastle@abdopub.com

SandCastle Level: Beginning

Featured Sight Words

before   boy

give   is

many   the

Shari rests before the soccer match.

The boy runs for the soccer ball.

The coach will give the boys advice.

Jan is ready to play soccer.

There are many players on Peg's team.

the

Dan carries the soccer ball under his arm.

The Match Is On!

Cindy waits before the soccer match.

She is ready to play.

The goalie on the other team is a boy.

He has saved many points.

Cindy wants to score the winning point.

She will give it a good try.